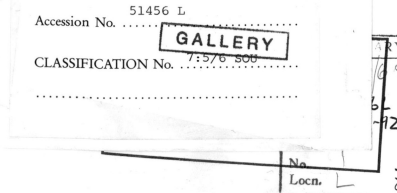

Bolton Museum
and Art Gallery
19 January to
23 February 1991

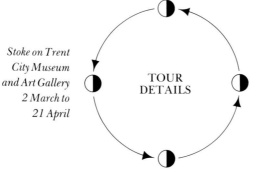

Stoke on Trent
City Museum
and Art Gallery
2 March to
21 April

TOUR
DETAILS

Glynn Vivian
Art Gallery,
Swansea
8 June to
21 July

Mead Gallery,
University of Warwick,
Coventry
29 April to 1 June

FOREWORD

Like the Face of the Moon is an exhibition concerned with objectivity in art, and with the strange and disconcerting effect that this can have. It brings together paintings, drawings, prints and photographs ranging in date from the eighteenth century to the present day, and includes anatomical and botanical illustrations as well as photographs taken on voyages of exploration.

While most of the scientific work comes from the earlier period, all the exhibits have qualities that we traditionally associate with science: there is deliberate detachment, exact description. The approach is one of enquiry, or exploration. In effect, the exhibition shows the discovery of the world in art; in the earlier works, the discovery of nature, as a store of surprises. Later on, nature becomes the object of a more anxious attention, and, in more recent works, artists turn a questioning gaze on their familiar surroundings, and find a strangeness in them. In spite of these differences, however, there are common visual and formal qualities; this is art that dwells intensely on edges, where visibility ceases. It makes us acutely aware of the margins that limit our vision and – by implication – our understanding. There is a hauntingness, a sense of the enigmatic, that comes from this.

We are very grateful to Brendan Prendeville who has devised and selected this exhibition in response to an idea of Michael Harrison's and to all the lenders who have responded to the project with such generosity and imagination.

We would also like to express our gratitude to all those who have helped in preparing this exhibition, including Dr. Peter Agius, Janet Barnes, Malcolm Beasley, Anne Bukantas, Fiona Chambers, Roger Crawford, Rachel Duncan, Sara Elliott, Anne Goodchild, Lynne Green, Francis Greenacre, Dr. T. Hobbs, Niall Hobhouse, Martin Hopkinson, Ian Jeffrey, Gillian Kennedy,Caroline Krzesinska, Ian Lyle, Sandra Martin, Corinne Miller, Victoria Miro, Andrew Moore, Lorcan O'Neill, Alex Potts, Alison Redwood, Pamela Roberts, Michelle Saviour, William Schupbach, David Scrase, Tessa Sidey, Peyton Skipwith, Gregory Smith, Nicholas Usherwood, Philip Vainker, Helen Valentine and Stephen Wildman.

JOANNA DREW *Director, Hayward and Regional Exhibitions*
CAROLINE COLLIER *Exhibition Organiser*

6(iii) Ferdinand Bauer *Sterculia Grandiflora*

LIKE ○THE FACE *of* THE MOON

THE ART OF DISCOVERY

How strange that things should be as they are. Anyone might have that feeling at times, even when gazing at something quite familiar. A similar sense of estrangement is evoked in art, when artists use intensely objective methods and bring so clear an eye to bear that – as with much of the work in this exhibition – even the recognisable and familiar become as if unknown.

What often compensates for this feeling is the sense of wonder that comes from discovery; not unlike that recounted by scientists or explorers who have seen something for the first time. 'See', in this context, means both setting one's eyes on something and – perhaps after a moment of doubt – comprehending it: it comes into view and it falls into place. There is a good example of this in Galileo's account of his observation of the Moon through a telescope. The Moon was approaching the first quarter as 'into the luminous part there extended a great dark gulf in the neighbourhood of the lower cusp. When I had observed it for a long time and had seen it completely dark, a bright peak began to emerge, a little below its centre, after about two hours. Gradually growing, this presented itself in a triangular shape, remaining completely detached and separated from the lighted surface. Around it three other small points soon began to shine, and finally, when the moon was about to set, this triangular shape (which had meanwhile become more and more extended) joined with the rest of the illuminated region and suddenly burst into the gulf of shadow like a vast promontory of light...'[1]

There is art as well as science in this description, which comes from *The Starry Messenger*, of 1610. Earlier in that short book, Galileo had straightforwardly stated his findings that the Moon was not smooth, but rough and uneven, having mountains and valleys 'just like the earth's surface'. In the passage quoted, he continues to present his evidence for this, writing as factually and scrupulously as before, yet now in such a way as to create an image suggestive of his own dawning realisation – the wonder of discovery. He ends the paragraph by heightening his description still more, using similes that evoke a precise beauty: 'This part of the moon's surface, where it is spotted as the tail of a peacock is sprinkled with azure eyes, resembles those glass vessels which have been plunged while still hot into cold water and have thus acquired a crackled and wavy surface, from which they receive their common name of "ice-cups".'

This exhibition is concerned with visual art that creates an analogous sense of discovery, while using comparably objective means. Objectivity, in this context, implies a use of techniques that impose distance, but that allow a slow and patient familiarisation. The French poet Paul Valéry had something like this in mind when he wrote about examining an object and 'illuminating, one by one, the facets of my ignorance'. As his words imply, the thing so studied answers – must answer – to something in us. The answers – like the questions – change with time. Broadly, the exhibition presents three phases, and three kinds, of objectivity in art, from the eighteenth century to the present.

1. Disclosure, in Art and Science

'About twenty-five years since, I first saw the Moon through a telescope, which I now recollect must have been about two Days after the first Quarter; you will conclude how much struck a young Man conversant with Light, and Shade, must be with the Moon in this state; especially, as I was not taught to expect such clearness and expression, as is to be found near and upon the indented Edge; a few Days after I made a small Drawing, but the Moon being at the Full, I was not struck in the same manner, and I made no more attempts, till an accidental possession of a powerful Glass awakened my attention to this beautiful Object once more, and for several years I have lost few opportunities when the Atmosphere has exhibited the Object of my study and imitation.'
John Russell R.A., 1789.[2]

During the eighteenth century, visual art came to be more closely allied to science than it had ever been before, or than it has been since that time. This alliance was known and acknowledged. The great eighteenth century German poet, Goethe, who himself did important scientific work, praised the botanical artist Ferdinand Bauer for showing that it was possible to serve art and science at the same time. This was on the condition that the artist aimed strictly at accuracy; according to Goethe, the truth must come first, 'and through truth, beauty'.[3] The remark partly reflects a neo-classical preference for severity of style, as against the deliberately decorative effects of Dutch seventeenth century flower painting. But it also suggests a merging of aesthetic feeling and scientific curiosity: through accuracy and acuteness the artist could focus attention precisely on that which was seen as being intrinsically wonderful.

Cat no. **6**

There is no shortage of evidence that scientific enquirers felt a sense of wonder during this era of exploration and discovery – an age of sober artists and intoxicated scientists. In a letter of July 1799, written in Venezuela, the geographer and explorer Alexander von Humboldt exclaimed: 'What trees!.. pisang and a whole host of trees with enormous leaves and sweet smelling flowers as big as your hand, all utterly new to us. As for the colour of the birds and fishes – even the crabs are sky-blue and yellow! Up till now we've been running round like a couple of mad things; for the first three days we couldn't settle to anything; we'd find one thing, only to abandon it for the next. Bonpland keeps telling me he'll go out of his mind if the wonders don't cease soon'.[4] Nineteen years later, Sir Stamford Raffles wrote from Sumatra, describing a plant '...so distinct from every other flower, that I know not to what I can compare it – its dimensions will astonish you – it measured across from the extremity of the petals rather more than a yard, the nectarium was nine inches wide, and as deep; estimated to contain a gallon and a half of water, and the weight of the whole flower fifteen pounds... The inside of the cup is of an intense purple, and more or less densely yellow, with soft flexible spines of the same colour... It seems to be a flower unknown to most of the natives, as well as to naturalists.'[5]

Such excited letters home show that the activities of collecting and describing held high importance for scientists, and this had obvious consequences for visual art. During the eighteenth century, biological sciences underwent an enormous change, such that, in all fields of enquiry, artists increasingly were called on to assist the work of science. Scientific illustration did of course already have a long history, but now there was a new urgency, and a stringency; the botanical artist's work would be, in Goethe's words 'examined by a whole host of critical experts'. The greater the degree of unfamiliarity, the more need there was for exactness: the anatomist William Hunter wrote in 1774 that 'the slight manner of producing an effect' was acceptable when a 'subject is so well known, that a mere hint is enough to the imagination... But in anatomy, as in natural history, the subject is supposed to be new, or only imperfectly known; and the smaller parts are to be studied with care, as well as the larger masses'.[6] Hunter's words come from the preface to *The Human Gravid Uterus*; he would certainly have read the preface which the great Dutch anatomist Gottfried Albinus published with his own major anatomical work in 1749, and have found the (rather insistent) claim that the artist 'was instructed, directed, and as entirely ruled by me, as if he was a tool in my hands...'[7]

What was true in anatomy and in botany applied quite

generally, wherever art and science became associated. This extended to landscape, when artists like William Hodges and William Westall joined naval expeditions as recorders of topography, and faced an immediate audience not only of scientists but also of naval officers, who themselves were practised observers.[8] Such close critical attention might seem cramping; and yet some of the work that resulted is hypnotically fascinating. In fact, artists were partners rather than mere subordinates: scientists did the naming and describing, artists drew with this guidance. Nowhere was this close collaboration more evident than in the great scientific voyages of exploration, beginning with Cook's first expedition to the South Seas (1768–1771). Joseph Banks, a wealthy man with a deep commitment to science, and later to be President of the Royal Society (which promoted Cook's voyage), joined the expedition, bringing with him the botanist Dr Solander and two artists, one of whom, Sydney Parkinson, was to draw flora and fauna. In his journal, Banks described their work, using terms that did not present the artist as a mere instrument. 'We sat at the great table with the draughtsman directly across from us. We showed him how the drawings should be depicted and hurriedly made descriptions of all the natural history objects while they were still fresh...'[9] This took place at each landfall, as the expedition did its work of charting the islands and coastlines of the South Pacific. As each specimen was labelled and mounted, Parkinson did minimal drawings, with touches of colour, to serve as a basis for subsequent finished work. He added his own colour notes, for example: 'The petals and stamina white and the anthera yellow the buds ting'd wt green calyx gray green turning pale towards the edge the main stalk of the flower deep green the woody stalk sordid brown' (*Barringtonia Calyptrata*).'

What we notice in this description is a use of botanical terms to name parts. Between 1735 and 1758 Karl Linnaeus introduced and applied systems for classifying plants and animals and through this, most importantly, established the practice of naming each living thing by genus and species. Individuals could thus be defined both in their parts and as part of a greater whole, which both stimulated and assisted the work of collecting, since botanists like Solander – a pupil of Linnaeus – could now readily give each specimen its place in an expanding system of knowledge. This is not to say that all eighteenth century scientists were systematisers; the great French naturalist Buffon was a critic of Linnaeus' methods. But he, in his *Histoire Naturelle* (1749–1804, published in forty-four volumes, completed posthumously) showed a similar aspiration to comprehensiveness, and this was characteristic of eighteenth century biology, which, more specifically even than other fields of thought during the period, took inspiration from Newton.

What Newton had achieved for the first time was a definition of 'laws of nature' that treated the earth uniformly with the heavens. His was a God who dwelt in nature, as its organising principle. This attitude, brought to bear on terrestrial life, gave the scientific study of nature a new kind of cultural significance and made its smallest discoveries appear momentous. In 1771, Linnaeus wrote of his impatience to see the new specimens brought back by 'my pupil Solander', in terms that are characteristic of this period: 'I cannot but presume ... as Peru and Chili [have proved to be] so rich, that in the South-sea islands, as great an abundance of rarities have remained in concealment, from the beginning of the world, to reward the labours of our illustrious voyagers. I see these things now but afar off. If our travellers should take another trip, I shall have seen them as Moses saw Canaan'.[10] In an imaginary sense, these scientists and explorers were re-creating the world, through mapping its regions and describing its populations (and doing so in their own image, too, particularly with the naming of places: 'New Holland' – later Australia – came still more incongruously to contain 'New South Wales').

Cat nos. **1–5**

The means whereby Linneaus and others eager for promised knowledge expected to see it was through illustration: Banks intended to publish a complete set of engravings, and after Parkinson's death employed artists including Frederick Nodder to complete finished watercolours for engravers. A set of plates was made and proofed, though not finally published. That notwithstanding, it was a project very much of its time. Whether through employment at the great botanic gardens of the period, or through work for anatomists and natural historians, or in publishing ventures of their own (as with Stubbs and Bewick), artists represented nature in terms of organised knowledge. The epitome of this ordered visual display of specimens was the museum, itself an outcome of the activities of collecting and of systematic description. In the later eighteenth

1(i) Frederick Nodder *Deplanchea Tetraphylla*

20(iii) George Stubbs *The Anatomy of the Horse* 1756–8

century, the surgeon and anatomist John Hunter created a museum in which specimens were chosen and presented so as to show anatomical continuities between different animal species.[11] He also commissioned paintings of wild animals from Stubbs and Agasse, which he used to complement his display of specimens. In this one may see a point of fundamental importance: eighteenth century investigation of nature worked mainly at the level of ordinary perception, and in terms either of externals or – as with skeleton and musculature – with closely underlying and conforming structures. This meant that a painting could fittingly keep company with zoological and anatomical displays, provided the artist painted the image with an appropriate clarity.

While artists participated in the work of science as specialist illustrators wherever this was required, it was chiefly in Britain that science came to have a wider effect on the art of painting. Partly, this took a traditional form, through the continuing study of anatomy: John Hunter's brother William was professor of anatomy at the newly-established Royal Academy. But the painter George Stubbs did his own anatomical work, and produced two extraordinary publications.[12] He painted wild animals for William Hunter's collection, as he had done for John's; and, like Joseph Wright of Derby, he did work for members of that important group of scientific enquirers, the Lunar Society.[13] The landscapists Hodges and Westall, mentioned previously, went, respectively, with the Cook/Banks expedition and with Matthew Flinders' expedition, and in their work they set aside the conventions of neo-classical landscape so as to give an exact account of coastal terrain.[14] Their attempts to define the unfamiliar led them to make formal separations which rendered the landscape as a relatively stark array of objects – as in contemporary paintings from nature like those of Thomas Jones. Though deprived of Claudian grace, such Cat nos. **16, 17** paintings can bear a family resemblance to the neo-classical *figure* painting of their own time, in so far as a sense of the frieze or shallow relief is common to both.

What recurs in everything considered so far is that the picture approximates to a display. Objects are presented frontally and in visual isolation, while a particularising attention is brought to bear on their parts. There is an overall simplicity or bluntness, combined with a fine texture of detail. The requirement for this in illustrations prompted engravers further to refine their technique; what they now offered, as William Hunter wrote in the preface to his *Gravid Uterus*, was a 'universal language [which] conveys clearer ideas of most natural objects, than words can express'.[15] This, as well as telling us something about the power of illustration, betrays its limits. Pictures go beyond words, in the sense intended, only when words are engaged essentially in a naming of parts; images refine and fill out the verbal description on which they depend – which is far from saying that they have no autonomy.

Cat no. **19**

In style, this scientific art shows a mixture of idealisation and realism that is found elsewhere in art of the period. The austere simplicity of presentation combined with fine tonal description gives a sense of realities soberly disclosed. Nothing conforms more closely with this formulation than John Russell's stipple engravings of the moon 'from his original drawings carefully measured by a micrometer'. In the second of these 'lunar planispheres' he employs a kind of scientific licence, since, impossibly, light falls obliquely across the entire surface, which gives him the artistic opportunity to dwell recurrently on areas where light debates with darkness. The moon could serve to epitomise all these science-related images in so far as, visually, they are suspended in a void, and studied as if from afar in terms of the passage of light. In botanical work, the globe-like forms of fruiting bodies which might formerly have been considered unbeautiful, received appreciative interpretation, particularly in the hands of Ferdinand Bauer, who used fine watercolour stippling to build larger forms from a regular microstructure. His paintings employ a principle of growth abstracted, rather than copied, from the exotic plants. Their voluptuousness becomes ethereal.

Cat no. **18**

Cat nos. **6, 7**

In terms of anatomy, Hunter/Van Rymsdyk and George Stubbs represent two relative extremes. Both present their subjects in a kind of lunar suspense and employ fine tonal modelling. In some plates of the *Gravid Uterus*, however, the woman's torso is shown with the limbs severed, and Hunter's aspiration to realism is evident also in his adherence, where possible, to actual size. One plate shows a window reflected on the surface of the darkened amniotic sac, and Hunter remarks on this realistic detail in his commentary. Realism was a matter of policy: in his preface, Hunter distinguishes between two

17 Thomas Jones *Scene near Naples* 1783

approaches to anatomy, one of which (his own) being 'finished from a view of one subject', while the other uses several, to achieve clarity of presentation. 'The one shows the object, and gives perception; the other only describes, or gives an idea of it.' Stubbs certainly used many subjects for his *Anatomy of the Horse*, and the general arrangement of his work is schematic (he follows the example of Albinus).[16] Additionally, he shows the figures without a background, and compresses the foreshortening. Both anatomists, however, follow the practice of injecting the veins with wax, so that they stand out in effigy of life. The impression of lifelikeness is greater with Hunter/Van Rymsdyk, which is consistent with the subject: life itself, traced back through its gestation. Yet, as with Stubbs, the realism here is sculptural; there is disclosure to light by a successive removal of layers. We know that what we see is not really life itself, but the shell or form of it. This we gaze on with rapt attention, rather like the people in Joseph Wright of Derby's *A Philosopher Giving that Lecture on the Orrery...*, who watch a clockwork model of the solar system 'in which a lamp is put in place of the Sun'.

Cat no. **20**

Cat nos. **23**, **24** The mezzotints after other paintings by Wright in this exhibition similarly show his characteristic use of light to suggest inward illumination. In *A Blacksmith's Shop*, an ageing man ponders, while young men work and children play; in *Miravan*, the tomb-breaker recoils when he is shown an inscription that contains a curse. The strangeness in all these images – with Van Rymsdyk, Stubbs, Wright – comes from a conjoining of opposites, in terms both of existence and of consciousness: lifelikeness and deathly stillness; disclosing light and enfolding darkness; bold enquiry and troubled conscience.

2. Apprehending Nature

'A widely extended and apparently interminable plain stretches from the southern base of the lofty granitic crest which in the youth of our planet, when the Caribbean gulf was formed, braved the intrusion of the waters... [T]he traveller sees before him steppes receding [to the] far horizon. Neither hill nor cliff rises, like an island in the ocean, to break the uniformity of the boundless plain; only here and there broken strata of limestone ... appear noticeably higher than the surroundings. "Banks" is the name given to them by the natives, as if language instinctively recalled the more ancient epoch when these plateaux were shoals and the steppes themselves were the bottom of a great Mediterranean sea... Estranged from the destinies of mankind and riveting attention only to the present moment, this corner of the earth appears as a wild theatre for the free development of animal and vegetable life.'
Alexander von Humboldt, *Aspects of Nature*, 1808.[17]

'We know that gentians grow on the Alps, and olives on the Appenines; but we do not enough conceive for ourselves that variegated mosaic of the world's surface which a bird sees in its migration, that difference between the district of the gentian and of the olive which the stork and the swallow see afar off as they lean upon the sirocco wind. Let us, for a moment, try to raise ourselves even above the level of their flight, and imagine the Mediterranean lying beneath us like an irregular lake, and all its ancient promontaries sleeping in the sun: here and there an angry spot of thunder, a grey stain of storm, moving upon the burning field; and here and there a fixed wreath of white volcano smoke, surrounded by its circle of ashes; but for the most part a great peacefulness of light, Syria and Greece, Italy and Spain, laid like pieces of a golden pavement into the sea-blue...'
John Ruskin, *The Stones of Venice*, 1853.[18]

I t is a mark of the difference between eighteenth and nineteenth century biology that, while Buffon gave illustration an important place in his *Histoire Naturelle*, Darwin illustrated *The Origin of Species* (1859) with only a single diagram. What Darwin described could not readily be pictured; although nineteenth century artists and illustrators did depict scenes of conflict in nature, no picture could show what Darwin summarised as 'the accumulation of slight modifications of structure or instinct, each profitable to the individual under its conditions of life'.[19]

In botany and in other fields the work of collecting continued, but in the nineteenth century other kinds of scientific enquiry came to predominate; scientists came increasingly to study nature from the inside, as it were, in terms of autonomous functions. These did not readily reduce to sets of objects that could be exhibited or illustrated, and so science and art lost the closely complementary relationship so far described. But science continued to be important to artists who studied nature and, in Britain especially, art itself developed a concern with living processes.

However, there is at least one case where these changes in artistic and scientific outlook can be studied jointly. Sir Charles Bell, important for his work in physiology, was also an anatomist and drew the illustrations for his own and his brother John's publications. He also wrote a book on the anatomy of expression which, after its publication in 1806, went into several editions; and he gave lectures and lessons on anatomy which artists attended – one of them was Charles Landseer, a brother of Edwin. Bell was expressly critical of the practice of constructing an ideal anatomy, such as we see in Stubbs' book of 1766. This, it has been remarked, would not have been much use to a veterinary surgeon, since the viscera were omitted, and little was shown of the arterial system.[20] Obviously the artifice of peeling the body in successive layers could not allow the artist to depict, in Bell's words, 'the peculiar course and turnings of the [blood] vessels' – woven as these are through all the body's systems.[21] They could be uncovered, and drawn, only through deep investigation of particular parts.

That is what Bell's drawings show, exactly as on the anatomist's table. He even makes us disconcertingly aware that

Cat no. **28**

Cat nos. **46, 47**

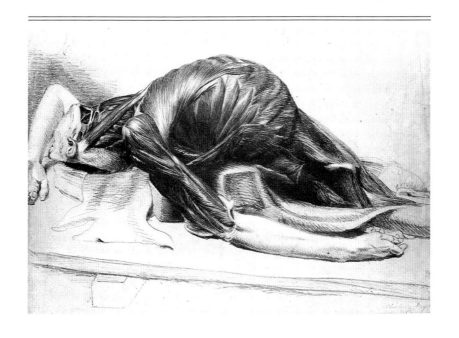

47 Charles Landseer *Right Lateral view of trunk and neck of écorché corpse supine*

61 James Ward *A Young Bull* 1811

what we see is – or was – an individual (nature creates only individuals and, rather than construct a type, Bell chooses a body that shows 'the most natural and usual distribution of vessels').[22] Hunter/Van Rymsdyk would seem to offer a closer comparison than Stubbs, since their images show a high degree of physical realism. But, hardly less than Stubbs, they give primacy to pure vision; light, as it closely models surfaces and textures, evenly discloses all things. Bell's drawings, which are fluently linear rather than modelled, show not a peeling back of layers so much as a series of excavations, sharply focussed so as to pick out veins and arteries. It is not simply that these drawings use a technique appropriate to the task; there is a degree of empathy in Bell's style, just as there is an emotion informing his and his brother's physiological descriptions.[23]

Similar points emerge in the case of animal painting, where it is appropriate to compare Stubbs' work with that of James Ward. Ward's painting of *A Young Bull* (1811) shows a general debt to Stubbs in its tonal carving and in the attention it pays to anatomy. The profile view is a convention maintained since Buffon, and used by British painters in pictures of prize cattle – like Stubbs' own *Lincolnshire Ox*. Classical antiquity has a bearing too, since the prominent veins owe something to the example of the Elgin Marbles.[24] But through and despite all that there is a quality of brute presence in Ward's painting such as we do not find in Stubbs.

Cat no. **61**

Cat no. **22**

Materiality was very much an issue during this era of agricultural improvement; after 1800, Sir Humphrey Davy lectured and published on agricultural chemistry, and the emphasis on production is evident in the practice of depicting 'improved' cattle alongside the men who fed them.[25] However, Stubbs suggests the massiveness of the Lincolnshire Ox by the rather wonderful expedient of putting a fowl beside it, while letting the man stand by urbanely, hat in hand, as the third part of the frieze. Compare with that the work of a near-contemporary of Ward, Thomas Weaver, who enhances the bulk of his cattle and shows the men solemnly or gleefully preparing fodder.

Cat no. **62**

Ward's bull was probably one of Lord Ribblesdale's Gisburn herd of wild cattle, painted in the course of his *Gordale Scar* commission (1811–1814).[26] The huge painting, and the studies for it, were based on thoroughgoing objective study.

Cat no. **60**

However, Ward freely distorted the given view in order to enhance its effect: he used the conventions of pictorial realism for a visionary purpose. Through several oil studies he rehearsed and developed his orchestration of the elements: the earth opens, water pours out, clouds roll overhead and animal life appears.

Although it is still a matter here, as in the eighteenth century cases, of a visual enquiry into nature, the questions being asked are different ones: what produces and sustains life? how is the natural world composed, how are its parts necessary to each other, and how are we a necessary part of it? These are not a sceptic's questions, but invitations to faith and imagination; they entail a 'willing suspension of disbelief', as a sequel to doubt. That is quite obvious with visionary art; but even in the topographic work of landscapists like Danby and Cotman the discipline of lucid naturalism may carry a visionary implication. We find these artists returning to views of river valleys or rock clefts, as yielding intimations of the Earth's inner structure. John Martin offered a more deliberately expressive account of this in a watercolour of the Wye Valley. And in 1838 a frontispiece by him appeared in Mantell's *Wonders of Geology*, which showed ancient reptiles doing battle in a primaeval tropical landscape.[27]

Cat nos. **35–37**
Cat nos. **31–34**

Cat no. **50**

In Britain, the question of origins came to have a hold on the scientific and artistic imagination even before Darwin. Pioneering work on the history of the Earth had been done in other countries – notably by Buffon – but it was in Britain that geology attained a central place in the study of nature, particularly through the work of Charles Lyell (*Principles of Geology*, 1830–3), which was to be of great importance to Darwin. Scientists might now, in describing nature, range widely across time and space; in 1834, Alexander von Humboldt outlined a scheme for his book *Cosmos*: 'The whole physical astronomy – our solid earth, inside, outside, the electromagnetism of the interior. Volcanism, i.e. the reaction of the interior of the planet on its surface. The structure of the solid masses. A little geology, the sea, the atmosphere, climates, organisms, geography of plants. Geography of animals, the human races and languages whose physical organisation (the production of sounds) is regulated by the intellect...'[28]

Where, in all this material existence, is there room for a

TOP: **50** John Martin *The Wye Valley* 1844   *BOTTOM:* **25** Unknown Eighteenth Century Artist *The Inner Crater of a Volcano* c1800–1810

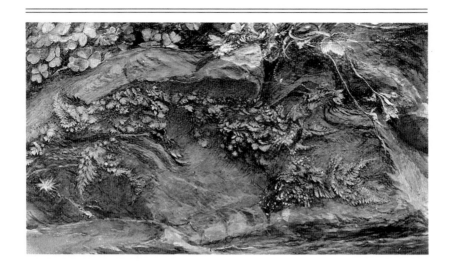

56 John Ruskin *Study of Moss, Fern and Wood Sorrel and a Rocky Bank* 1875–9

Creator? In Britain, at the time when Humboldt wrote his letter, a number of scientists were trying, expressly, to make materiality sustain the Deity. The Earl of Bridgewater, who died in 1829, had bequeathed money so that scientists might be commissioned to write, from within their specialisms, 'on the Power, Wisdom and Goodness of God, as manifested in the Creation'. Sir Charles Bell was one of them, and he published his treatise on *The Hand* in 1833, while the treatise on geology was written by Dr Buckland.[29]

Ruskin knew Buckland at Oxford, and Ruskin's own deep interest in this subject and in the scientific study of nature generally, are well known. While these concerns informed Ruskin's writing on art, they did so as part of a sustained effort by him to persuade his contemporaries to see nature as something *necessary* to them, in a sense not merely utilitarian. His books contain many passages on natural phenomena whose informed intensity alone gives a heightened sense of the thing described; but there is always another level too, whereby he draws this objectified nature into a fabric of religious meanings. He sees nature in terms of the Creation and in terms, therefore, of hope and fear. The undulating forms of 'slaty crystallines' 'bear upon them the symbol of perpetual fear': a memory of the forces of creation, and of forces yet to be unleashed, as in a passage from Jeremiah, 'I beheld the mountains and lo they *trembled*; and all the hills *moved lightly*'.[30] What Ruskin offers in *Modern Painters* is a detailed *narration* of nature, in which he recounts the life of earth, air, water and vegetation, as comprising numerous interacting and interdependent agencies – as opposed to the 'multitudinous formalisms of the laws of Nature'.[31]

Ruskin's words no doubt allude to eighteenth century symmetries. But the science of Ruskin's own time produced 'laws' of its own, and descriptions, too, that are quite as fearful as his. Darwin concluded *The Origin of Species* by inviting the reader 'to contemplate an entangled bank, clothed with many plants of many kinds, with birds singing on the bushes, with various insects flitting about, and with worms crawling through the damp earth, and to reflect that these elaborately constructed forms, so different from each other in so complex a manner have all been produced by laws acting around us... [F]rom the war of nature, from famine and death, the most exalted object which we are capable of conceiving, namely, the production of the higher animals, directly follows...'[32]

For Ruskin, however, nature is finally unexplainable, opaque: 'No words, that I know of, will say what these mosses are'. Not even such words as only he was capable of finding: 'creatures full of pity, covering with strange and tender honour the scarred disgrace of ruin'.[33] The image is highly characteristic and evokes his drawings, where vegetation finds holds and

Cat no. **56**

paths in rock crevices. He imagines nature as being made up of strands plaited together, and his pictures show how one form of life winds out with another, as in his writing, which so often resembles Biblical genealogies. The whole point is, our knowing of nature is not detached, but involving. Infinitely so: 'For a stone, when it is examined, will be found a mountain in miniature. The fineness of nature's work is so great, that into a single block, a foot or two in diameter, she can compress as many changes of form and structure, on a small scale, as she needs for her mountains on a large one...'[34]

This minuteness is characteristic of all Ruskinian and Pre-Raphaelite naturalism. There is sometimes an unfulfillable longing in it, of a kind that led Thomas Seddon and Holman

Cat no. **59**

Cat nos. **44**, **45**

Hunt to travel to the Middle East in order to find a still more searching light, a more deeply buried past, and ancient, planetary landscapes. In order also to see beyond the confines of the present: in 1857, a critic remarked of Hunt's painting *The Sphinx, Gizeh* 'the desert is the true subject, over which we are desired to look with the sphinx, who has been regarding the same for thirty centuries'.[35]

3. Remote Sensing

'Hastily dressing, I went on deck, and saw a gleaming white floating island near the horizon. The sun, already high in the heavens, for we were in a latitude of 65° South, was touching it caressingly, causing it to stand out in vivid contrast to the cobalt ocean and the sombre gloom of the distance. As I gazed at the wonderful and, to me, novel sight, I felt that we were at last really at the threshold of that Great White South...'
Herbert Ponting, *The Great White South*, 1921

pace exploration has yielded photographs of the Earth seen above the lifeless surface of the moon. The Earth has its own barren landscapes, and in recent times artists and explorers have been attracted to these outer limits. Partly, their work has consisted in adding to knowledge, finding new kinds of beauty. But additionally it has fulfilled a peculiarly modern desire to get outside the world; or, more fundamentally, to escape from an habitual and blinkered perception.

Cat no. 84

A limit must partly be defined in relation to a centre, and the geographical centre in this case has been Europe. The recent history of exploration is inseparable from that of European empires and migrations: exploration is an activity of the powerful – Cook's voyages served the interests of naval power as well as those of pure science.[36] The British tradition of combined naval and scientific expeditions continued into the twentieth century, with Scott's Polar exploration of 1910–12. Scott's ship the *Terra Nova* was particularly well equipped for scientific investigation and the photographer with the party,

Cat no. 88

Herbert Ponting, took pictures of scientists at work. In his book *The Great White South* (1921) he stressed the scientific reasons for going to the Polar region. Yet the title itself betrays a different motive, an imaginary objective: it suggests a non-human extreme, a definitive outer limit.

Ponting was a professional, working with a view to publication, and had an audience in mind. Thus there are winsome images of penguins and seals, and impressive towering icebergs. This calculatedness can become obtrusive, particulary if set against the rather more factual work of Frank Hurley, photographer with the Shackleton expedition of 1914–17. Yet Ponting's artistry was considerable and his comprehensive account of the expedition remains compelling, even as – photography being what it is – we become aware of the distance that separates his time from ours. Now, we notice not just the vulnerability of the explorers but their self-containment. The activities of measuring and observing, in this conspicuously inhospitable environment, have an air of slight absurdity.

Ultimately, the scientist's exact measurements are like any other method of description: they impose a pattern. Scientists are of course mindful of this and try to make nature speak for itself, by designing instruments which respond directly and passively to natural processes. The camera is to some extent an instrument of this kind and can be put to scientific use. More to the point, Ponting himself observed and recorded natural processes such as the formation of ice, both with his camera and in writing. In his book he describes how, as the cold wind struck the warmer water, it created vapour which, 'as it condensed, froze in the air, and fell back in minute particles of ice as soon as the wind subsided. Then again, when the sea was still, needle-like crystals could be seen forming under water, and tiny flat crystals also; these would float to the surface and quickly freeze to each other, forming thin frozen disks...'[37] Ponting's photographs of this were not in any sense 'scientific'; the point is, rather, that a photograph could, more effectively than a drawing or print, represent environmental change. In this case, it could freeze the freezing process; or, as with his photo of a seal sliding from an ice-edge, serve to illustrate Darwinian natural selection, as no drawing could.[38]

Even if the subject of a photograph is static, however, change is evident through the camera's photochemical registering of light. Indeed, it is precisely in the absence of movement that light, besides letting us see, may make itself seen; provided the photographer appreciates the passivity of the camera, lets light do the work. Among Frank Hurley's photographs is a study of an unoccupied ship's cabin, receiving the gift of light – as it might have seemed, in a region of long nights.

The particular beauty of some early work suggests that photographers had remained mindful of the medium's fundamental properties, as in du Camp's pictures of Egyptian

79 Frank Hurley *Sphinx Rock near Rogers Head, Heard Island* 1929–31

94 Edwin Smith *Ambulatory of the Crypt, Canterbury* 1968

monuments, where light falls down dark surfaces like luminous
dust catching on roughnesses and projections. Unlike Holman
Hunt and Seddon, whose paintings were efforts to bring the
Biblical past into the present, through sheer persistence of
attention, du Camp let age remain mute, closed in its granite.

Cat no. **40**

Though photography was itself an outcome of painting,
modern painters have had to take it into account, particularly if
they were realists. Some modern realist movements have
identified elements of style common to both media. In Germany
during the 1920s, the term *Neue Sachlichkeit* ('New Objectivity')
was used to define tendencies seen not only in painting, but also
in the work of photographers like Renger-Patzsch: an impassive
yet intense concern for the facts – *Sachen* – of visibility. More
recently, with equal self-effacement, American Photo-Realists
have painted faithful copies of commonplace photographs. But
more fundamental than style is the underlying principle of
objectification. This entails representing objects in such a way as
to make them appear independent of, and indifferent to,
human consciousness; dwelling in themselves.

Cat nos. **89–92**

A common subject for painters and photographers work-
ing in this spirit, is the play of sunlight on buildings; its passage
through their inner spaces. Edwin Smith was a particularly sens-
itive interpreter of church interiors, who generally used an old,
large-format camera, and timed exposures intuitively. Only
informed guesswork, in any case, would have enabled him to
achieve results like those we see in his picture of the Crypt at
Canterbury. Lit by dimly diffracted sunlight, it might put us in
mind of the passively receptive interior of a camera. The
movements of light, the Sun itself, and the long-standing
columns have no heed for us, go on without us. In a similar
spirit, the painter Algernon Newton studied disregarded urban
views. Typically, a solitary building or street receives sunlight on
walls or curtained windows. They are still as sundials, at rest in
themselves, often shown from an ignored aspect, where they
back onto canals – a city's unseen thoroughfares. They are
marked by neglect.

Cat nos. **93–96**

Cat no. **94**

Cat nos. **85, 86**

The feelings of melancholy and dissociation in these
images are nonetheless compatible with a yearning towards the
things shown. Only in expressly modernist kinds of realism do
we find a more radical estrangement; for example, in Photo-
Realist work by painters like Richard Estes and Chuck Close.

Cat nos. **69, 67**

85 Algernon Newton *The Backs of Houses, Harley Street* 1925

68 Robert Cottingham *Carl's* 1977

With Estes we again find images of buildings, but the views are main-street ones, so that their total desertedness is incongruous. It is not the sunlight that embodies time and change, but the scene itself, where the architecture is as ephemeral as the play of reflections, the street signs, the pieces of litter. If we were to walk down such a street, it would be with a purpose (if only to get to the end of it) and our eyes would select accordingly. Estes suspends purpose, and the universally sharp focus takes us into every distinct detail of architecture and signage. The whole scene appears not only empty, but senseless: its beauty is alien.

Like other Photo-Realists, Estes accentuates the purely visible, as against the substantial. Art that uses objectifying methods must always strike a balance in this respect, and we can certainly find cases where the emphasis is different. Not only is Estes' subject without substance, it lacks intrinsic qualities of any kind – which obviously was not the case with Newton, nor with Edwin Smith; nor with other photographers who had an exacting eye, such as Edward Weston. All of these wanted to own the thing they saw; not in the naive sense of possessing it, but through recognising it, in its strangeness and apartness, as something needed. Vision is intensified, but not exalted.

Cat no. **101**

That strikes a Christian note; there is certainly a religious aspect to some modern realism, perhaps most evident in the case of Stanley Spencer, an artist born in the nineteenth century, and nurtured by Pre-Raphaelitism, yet modern in his eroticism, as evident in his realist work as it is in his visionary painting. The eye takes in the awkwardness, recalcitrance and ugliness of objects or of flesh as an act of acceptance – or a test of faith. In outdoor views, near and distant objects are juxtaposed, walls and paths break into their elements; his famous nudes, uningratiating to the point of menace, overfill their allotted space.

Cat nos. **97–100**

An ambiguous acceptance, perhaps; but reminders of our mortality can never be wholly welcome. However, it is through reminding us that we too have bodies that these paintings avoid voyeurism. The same is true of Lucian Freud, whose figures are so often asleep or in a daze; pushed back from consciousness into materiality, on a sagging couch in an undecorated room. Mere bodies, they lie unowned, as abandoned flesh and bones, and we look down on them like their temporarily departed spirits. Through estrangement, we are aware of need.

Cat nos. **71–74**

67 Chuck Close *Self-Portrait* 1977

99 Stanley Spencer *Landscape in North Wales* 1938

71 Lucian Freud *Still Life with Sea Urchin* 1949

101 Edward Weston *Point Lobos* 1946

Conclusion: a Modern Point of View

◐ ○ ○ *'Empty the pond to get the fish.'*
Robert Bresson[39]

o look into life from the outside, to escape from habit, habituation – in order to become aware of them: these are themes or motifs in recent criticism, philosophy and art. Let things reveal themselves: 'Let us establish [an]... interest ... in the [things] themselves, not straightforwardly but rather as objects in respect of their "how" – that is, with our interest directed toward *how ... world – the* world – comes into being for us'.[40]

The German philosopher Edmund Husserl wrote those words in the late 1930s; shortly before that time, the photographer Edward Weston had described his use of the camera as a process of watching the world come into being: 'To pivot the camera slowly around watching the image change on the ground glass is a revelation, one becomes a discoverer, seeing a world through the lens. And finally the complete idea is there, and completely revealed. *One must feel definitely, fully, before the exposure*'.[41] And this requires the perception of a certain reticence in the objects themselves. Edwin Smith complained of the capitals at Vézelay that they were 'so got up to be looked at [that]... the sense of discovery, of seeing them when they are not seeing you, is impossible'.[42]

Much of the recent work presented here shows this preoccupation with a world that knows nothing of us. Rather than apprehending an underlying lawfulness, the modern imagination tends towards scepticism. A contemporary scientist is prepared to doubt whether 'general principles of biological organization' exist, and to imagine that, 'in this broadest sense, life has no meaning'.[43]

According to this view, our descriptions of the world tell us only of ourselves. We can only classify, make inventories, emptily. Beneath that, there is nothing. The Bechers' photographic inventories of buildings made to house mechanical functions appear to imply this. Cat no. **66**

This fascination with the experience of being a stranger to

39

the world is suggested in one of Valéry's prose poems:

'Nothing more singular to my eyes, this morning, than that objects should go on as they do, that "bodies fall", that there are things that look like laws, sure consequences, constancies, periodicities; that reasoning is really rather often valid.

This sensation of oddity was my waking creation... It was my response to things as they are, or as they become again – as if I had expected quite another world. Indeed ... as if it had lain within my grasp.

Assume such a waking, my astonishment: what could be the greatest surprise of all, when one's eyes opened?'[44]

BRENDAN PRENDEVILLE

NOTES

1. Quoted from *Discoveries and Opinions of Galileo*, tr. Stillman Drake, New York, 1957, p.33.
2. Letter of Feb. 19, 1789; quoted by W.F. Ryan in 'John Russell and Early Lunar Mapping', *Smithsonian Journal of History*, Vol.1, 1966, p.28.
3. Quoted in Wilfrid Blunt, *The Art of Botanical Illustration*, London 1950, p.200.
4. Translated and quoted in Douglas Botting, *Humboldt and the Cosmos*, London 1973, p.76.
5. Quoted by Mildred Archer in *Natural History Drawings in the India Office Library*, 1962, p.15.
6. For an account of Hunter's principal draughtsman, see J.L. Thornton, *Jan van Rymsdyk, Medical Artist of the Eighteenth Century*, Cambridge 1982. See also the essay by J.L. Jordanova in W.F. Bynum and R.S. Porter (eds.), *William Hunter and the Eighteenth Century Medical World*, Cambridge 1985.
7. The quotation is from the English edition of Albinus' *Tables* of human anatomy (original edition, 1747). The preface is printed in facsimile in Terence Doherty, *The Anatomical Work of George Stubbs*, London 1974, p.313ff.
8. See Bernard Smith, *European Vision and the South Pacific, 1768–1850*, Oxford 1960.
9. Quoted in Hank Ebes (compiler), *The Florilegium of Captain Cook's First Voyage to Australia, 1768–1771*, Sotheby's Australia 1988, p.9.
10. Quoted by James Britten in his introduction to a set of reproductions of some of the Banks prints, published 1900–05.
11. See Judy Egerton's essay 'Stubbs and the Scientists', in *George Stubbs, Anatomist and Animal Painter*, Tate Gallery 1976, p.31: 'Stubbs and the Hunters'.
12. *The Anatomy of the Horse*, 1766; *Comparative Anatomical Exposition of the Structure of the Human Body with that of a Tiger and a Common Fowl*, published 1804–06; uncompleted.
13. See David Fraser, 'Joseph Wright of Derby and the Lunar Society', in J. Egerton, *Wright of Derby*, Tate Gallery 1990, p.15ff.
14. See Bernard Smith, *op. cit.*, pp.3, 11–12.
15. The only one of his artists whom Hunter mentions by name in his preface is his principal engraver, Robert Strange.
16. Doherty, *op. cit.*, reproduces all the studies and engravings.
17. Translated and quoted in L. Kellner, *Alexander von Humboldt*, London 1963, pp.37–42.
18. *Op.cit.*, Book 2, Part 2, Ch.IV, 'The Nature of Gothic'.
19. *The Origin of Species*, Harmondsworth 1985, p.215; in connection with some issues raised here, see Alex Potts, 'Natural order and the Call of the Wild', *The Oxford Art Journal*, Vol.13, No.1, 1990, pp.12–33.
20. See Egerton, *op. cit.*, 1976, p.37, 'Stubbs and the Veterinarians'.
21. From preface to *Engravings of the Arteries;* quoted from 2nd. ed., 1806, p.8.
22. *Ibid.*, p.9.
23. John Bell complained that previous anatomists had too often used 'the language of hydraulics and hydrostatics ... in describing the living system'. *(Anatomy of the Human Body*, Vol.II, 3rd. ed., 1808, p.X.)
24. See Edward J. Nygren, *James Ward's 'Gordale Scar'*, Tate Gallery 1982, p.50.
25. See Demelza Spargo, *This Land is Our Land: Aspects of Agriculture in English Art*, Mall Galleries, London 1989.
26. Nygren, *op. cit., loc. cit.*
27. Reproduced in David Knight, *The Age of Science*, Oxford 1986, p.119.
28. Quoted in Kellner, *op. cit.*, p.201.
29. *The Hand; its Mechanism and Vital Endow-*

ments as *Evincing Design*, London 1833.

30. *Modern Painters*, Vol.IV, 1856; Part V, Ch.IX, sec.6.

31. *Ibid.*, Ch.VI, sec.6.

32. *The Origin of Species*, p.459; see also the similar passage on pp.125–6.

33. *Modern Painters*, Vol.V, 1860; Part VI, Ch.X, sec.24.

34. *Modern Painters*, Vol.IV; Part V, Ch.XVIII, sec.7.

35. See the entry by Judith Bronkhurst in *The Pre-Raphaelites*, Tate Gallery 1984, p.270.

36. In his *Account of the Voyages...*, 1773, John Hawkesworth emphasized contributions to knowledge, and made a point of praising the King's 'liberal motives' in promoting expeditions.

37. *The Great White South*, p.105.

38. Ponting also made a film in the Antarctic; a photograph shows him filming the bows of the ship breaking through ice.

39. Robert Bresson, *Notes on Cinematography*, tr. Jonathan Griffin, New York 1975, p.48.

40. Edmund Husserl, *The Crisis of the European Sciences and Transcendental Phenomenology*, tr. David Carr, Evanston 1970, p.144. Written 1934–8.

41. Edward Weston, article of 1930, quoted in Ian Jeffrey, *Photography, a Concise History*, London 1981, p.148.

42. Letter quoted by Olive Cook in the introduction to *Edwin Smith*, London 1984, p.10.

43. R.C. Lewontin, 'Fallen Angels'; review of *Wonderful Life* by S.J. Gould, *New York Review of Books*, June 14 1990, pp.3–7.

44. *Singularities II*, from the collection *Mixture*, 1939, in *Poems in the Rough*, tr. Hilary Corke, London 1970, p.53; punctuation as in original.

LIKE ◐ THE FACE *of* THE MOON

CATALOGUE

*The arrangement of the
catalogue in three sections
reflects the historical span of the
exhibition. Entries are under
artist (or, on occasion, under the
name of a project, where this is
collaborative), in alphabetical
order within each section.
Dimensions of works are given
in centimetres, height before
width. All works are on paper,
unless otherwise indicated.*

ARTISTS BORN BEFORE 1765

The Banks Illustrations

Sir Joseph Banks (1743–1820) paid for a botanist, Dr Solander, and two artists, Sydney Parkinson and William Hodges, to accompany him on Captain Cook's first voyage to the South Seas, 1768–1771. He planned to publish a set of botanical illustrations based on Parkinson's original drawings. Parkinson completed 280 finished drawings of flora, after his own originals, before his death in 1771; finished drawings were done subsequently by other artists (chiefly Nodder) using the remainder of his 955 drawings, in conjunction with the specimens. These were then engraved, between 1771 and 1784, though not published. In the last decade, some sets of prints were made by Editions Alecto (London), using the original plates. All of the original material is in the Botany Library (British Museum). Unlike Ferdinand Bauer, these artists tended to use bodycolour extensively, as well as watercolour. Plants are depicted actual size.

1 Deplanchea Tetraphylla
(i) Frederick Polydore Nodder
    watercolour and bodycolour
    54.5 x 35.5
(ii) Daniel MacKenzie
    engraving
    54.5 x 37.5

2 Syzgium Suborbiculare
Frederick Polydore Nodder
watercolour and bodycolour
54 x 37.5

3 Barringtonia Calyptrata
(i) Frederick Polydore Nodder
    watercolour and bodycolour
    54.5 x 37
(ii) Daniel MacKenzie
    engraving
    54.5 x 37.5
(iii) Sydney Parkinson
    pencil and watercolour
    54 x 37

4 Grevillea Glauca
John Frederick Miller
watercolour and bodycolour
54 x 35

5 Banksia Integrifolia
Charles White
engraving
50 x 32

Ferdinand Bauer (1760–1826)

Born in Austria; like his brother Francis, became internationally famous as a botanical draughtsman. Francis was employed by Joseph Banks at Kew; Ferdinand joined Mathew Flinders' expedition to Australia, in 1801, with the botanist Robert Brown. Shown here are some of the finished drawings that he made, starting in 1813, with the intention of illustrating Brown's descriptions. He engraved only fifteen before returning to Vienna, where he completed the drawings. Plants are actual size, or else to scale.

6
(i) **Cycas Media**
52.5 × 36
(ii) **Cycas Media**
52.6 × 35.8
(iii) **Sterculia Grandiflora**
52.4 × 35.4
(iv) **Sterculia Grandiflora**
52.4 × 35.6
(v) **Wolffia Lycioides**
51.9 × 34.8
watercolour
THE TRUSTEES OF THE BRITISH MUSEUM (NATURAL HISTORY) BOTANY LIBRARY

7 Norfolk Island
pencil
36.3 x 26.1
THE TRUSTEES OF THE BRITISH MUSEUM (NATURAL HISTORY) BOTANY LIBRARY

Thomas Bewick (1753–1828)

Famous as a wood engraver, and for his *General History of Quadrupeds* (1790).

8 The Whitley Large Ox, 1789
etching with some line engraving and aquatint
17.2 x 27.5
AGRICULTURAL ECONOMICS UNIT, OXFORD

Peter Brown (active 1766–1791)

Exhibited paintings of natural history subjects at the Royal Academy; by 1783, botanical painter to the Prince of Wales.

9 An Exotic Fish
watercolour and gouache on vellum
23.8 x 30.2
HAZLITT, GOODEN & FOX LTD.

Charles Collins (d. 1744)

10 A Pigeon 1741
gouache
53.8 x 37.3
LEEDS CITY ART GALLERIES

J S Gautier D'Agoty (fl. c. 1770)

Member of a family of anatomical and botanical artists.

11 Plate from **Essai d'Anatomie,** showing muscles at back of head
mezzotint
40.3 x 31.5
WELCOME INSTITUTE LIBRARY, LONDON

Georg Dyonis Ehret (1710–1770)

The drawing represents Ehret's first idea for Trew's *Plantae Selectae*, Nuremberg 1750–73, engraved by J.J. Hind.

12 Glory Lily (*Gloriosa Superba L.*)
watercolour and gouache on vellum
46.9 x 32.9
HAZLITT, GOODEN & FOX LTD

Impey Collection, possibly Bhawani Das (fl. c. 1780)

Between 1777 and 1783, when Lady Mary Impey (1749–1818) was living in Calcutta as wife of the Chief Justice, Sir Elijah Impey, she commissioned a large quantity of natural history illustrations from local artists. She also kept a menagerie. The drawings are now dispersed. Three artists were employed, all of them trained in the Mughal miniaturist tradition; the signatures on the Wellcome drawings appear to belong to the artist named above (the others were Zayn-al-Din and Ram Das). The animals are depicted life-size, and in the case of the snakes, lengths are noted in the inscription.

13 Snakes:
(i)   **King Cobra** 1782
    59.3 x 45.4
(ii) **Brown and pale yellow snake** 1782
    46.1 x 59.1
(iii) **Green snake**
    45.6 x 66.5
watercolour
WELLCOME INSTITUTE LIBRARY, LONDON

14 Insects:
(i)   **Cricket**
    45.2 x 33
(ii) **Black beetle**
    32 x 45.5
watercolour
WELLCOME INSTITUTE LIBRARY, LONDON

15 Fish:
(i)   **Chanda Fish depicted in 2 versions** 1783
    48 x 65.4
(ii) **Pahali fish** 1783
    48.8 x 65
watercolour
WELLCOME INSTITUTE LIBRARY, LONDON

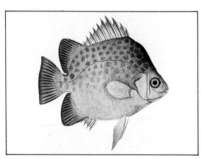

15(ii)

Thomas Jones (1742–1803)

Welsh-born landscapist who travelled and painted in Italy, 1776–1783; his modern reputation rests particularly on the small oil sketches that he painted in Naples.

16 A Hilltop near Naples 1782
oil on paper
14 x 21.5
BIRMINGHAM CITY MUSEUMS AND ART GALLERY

17 Scene near Naples 1783
oil on paper
24.1 x 34.6
THE SYNDICS OF THE FITZWILLIAM MUSEUM, CAMBRIDGE

John Russell (1745–1806)

RA who made his living as a portraitist in pastel. Was a keen amateur astronomer, in contact with leading scientists like Sir William Herschel; specialized in observation of the moon, which he first drew in 1764. Careful observation, drawing and measurement enabled him eventually to produce large pastel drawings (1795; Museum of the History of Science, Oxford, and Birmingham City Museum and Art Gallery) and an engraved adjustable globe, called *Selenographia*, in 1797. The two stipple engravings shown here are the plates from his *Lunar Planispheres* of 1805–6. Stipple was a fine etching process used especially in contemporary botanical illustration.

18

(i) **Plate 1** shows the full moon, '... Engraved by John Russell esq RA from his original drawings carefully measured by a micrometer...' 1805
line engraving and stipple
68 x 48.2

(ii) **Plate 2** shows the 'same view... as to libration, but with the rays of the sun falling *obliquely* upon it.. [this being something which in reality] cannot be true of the whole moon at once...' 1806
line engraving and stipple
68.2 x 48.5

WELLCOME INSTITUTE LIBRARY, LONDON

Jan Van Rymsdyk (fl. 1750–1789)

Artist and medical illustrator, employed by William Hunter over a period of 20 years, chiefly for *The Anatomy of the Human Gravid Uterus*; also drew for other eighteenth century anatomical and obstetric atlases. With his son Andrew Van Rymsdyk, illustrated the collection of the British Museum (*Museum Brittanicum*, 1778, 1791). Hunter intended to illustrate, in several stages and as accurately as possible, the growth of the foetus in the womb. Sometimes, the illustrations are also meant to show the causes of the failure of a pregnancy (as in Plate XII). Accordingly, Van Rymsdyk's drawings represent finely

19 The Anatomy of the Human Gravid Uterus

(i) **Drawing for Plate XII, J Van Rymsdyk**
red chalk on light green wash
31.6 x 47.3; the drawing shows a 9 month old foetus in the womb

(ii) **Plate XII, J Mitchel**
copper plate engraving
31.6 x 47.3; after Van Rymksdyk's drawing

(iii) **Drawing for Plate XXVI fig IV, J Van Rymsdyk**
red chalk
16.8 x 17.8; drawing of the womb opened to show 5 month old foetus seen through the amnion

(iv) **Four drawings for Plate XXXIII, figs I–IV, J Van**

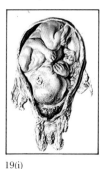

19(i)   19(iv)   19(iv)   19(iv)

and with great sensitivity the interrelationship of foetus and surrounding tissues. Hunter could thus confidently conclude his description of Plate XII with the remark that 'the situation, and the several parts of the child, require no explanation.' This called for skill on the artist's part, and for careful preparation by the surgeon. These images are fascinating but also disquieting, and not only through their concern with life and death: while the drawings present the foetus intact, and with an effect of tenderness, they show only parts of the mother, sometimes truncated – using the same realism.

Rymsdyk (mounted together)
red chalk
Fig i 6.2 x 1.18, Fig ii 6 x 12.5, Figs iii & iv 18 x 12.5; the plate as a whole shows six figures of three different abortions, at or about 9 weeks (figs i and ii) or 8 weeks. Each drawing shows placenta and foetus.

(v) **Three drawings for Plate XXXIII, figs V & VI, J Van Rymsdyk (mounted together)**
red chalk
Fig v 3.7 x 4.9, Fig vi 3.7 x 5.3, Fig vi 6 x 6
THE LIBRARIAN, GLASGOW UNIVERSITY

George Stubbs (1724–1806)

Father a leather-dresser in Liverpool. Trained as a portraitist; studied anatomy at York with John Burton and drew for his *Essay towards a Complete New System of Midwifery* 1751.

Began dissections for the *Anatomy of the Horse* in 1756, finished the drawings in 1758. He followed the most modern example: Albinus' *Tables of Human Anatomy*, published in English Edn. 1749. His procedure was to add the muscles to a previously drawn and traced skeleton. The drawings came to the RA as part of Charles Landseer's bequest, and are of two kinds: those done directly, in steep perspective, and finished drawings, like those shown here, which are synthesised from many working drawings. Stubbs made his own engravings, and the work was published in 1766. In 1795 he started work on *Comparative Anatomical Exposition*, which he also engraved, but died before he could complete it.

20 **The Anatomy of the Horse**
(i) **Finished Study for the Ninth Anatomical Table**
1756–58
graphite
34.2 x 18.4
(ii) **Finished Study for the Thirteenth Anatomical Table** 1756–58
graphite
34.2 x 18.4

In addition to three views of the skeleton – side, front and rear, with both the latter angled slightly, and as if in motion – Stubbs showed five stages of dissection for each of the same views. The above drawings, mounted together show fourth and third stages.

(iii) **Finished Study for the Third Anatomical Table**
1756–58
graphite
35.8 x 18.1
(iv) **Finished Study for the Third Skeleton Table**
1756–58
graphite
35.8 x 18.1
(v) **Finished Study for the Tenth Anatomical Table**
1756–58
graphite
35.6 x 19.4

The last two mounted together; the tenth table is the deepest stage from this view.
ROYAL ACADEMY OF ARTS

21 A Horse frightened by a Lion 1788
etching with mixed method engraving
23.5 x 32.7
THE HUNTERIAN ART GALLERY, UNIVERSITY OF GLASGOW

George Townley Stubbs (1756–1815)

Engraver, son of George Stubbs.

22 The Lincolnshire Ox dated Jan 20 1798
hand-coloured engraving
61 x 73.7
After George Stubbs' painting of 1790. In that year
'this uncommon animal' was brought to London for
exhibition. The print is dedicated to Sir Joseph
Banks, President of the Royal Society.
AGRICULTURAL ECONOMICS UNIT, OXFORD

Joseph Wright of Derby (1734–1797)

Portraitist; also painted a number of pictures with themes bearing on contemporary science, learning and literature. He was closely associated with members of the Lunar Society, a group which held monthly meetings during the 1770s to conduct scientific experiments and to discuss topics of concern to science and industry.

23 A Blacksmith's Shop, 1771
Richard Earlom, after Joseph Wright of Derby
mezzotint
60.6 x 43.2
THE HUNTERIAN ART GALLERY, UNIVERSITY OF GLASGOW

24 Miravan Breaking Open the Tomb of his Ancestors
Valentine Green, after Joseph Wright of Derby
mezzotint
50.4 x 35.5
THE HUNTERIAN ART GALLERY, UNIVERSITY OF GLASGOW

Unknown Eighteenth Century Artist

(Formerly attributed to William Hodges)

25 The Inner Crater of a Volcano c1800–1810
The scene has been identified as Vesuvius
oil on canvas
100.5 x 127
ROYAL PAVILION, ART GALLERY AND MUSEUMS, BRIGHTON

Unknown German Artist (fl. c. 1780)

The sheet comes from a group of drawings probably executed in the Solnhofen region of Germany.

26 Jurassic Fossils in Limestone
watercolour heightened with body colour
17 x 37.2
HAZLITT, GOODEN & FOX LTD

ARTISTS BORN BETWEEN 1765 AND 1870

John James Audubon (1780–1851)

Pupil of David. His great work was *The Birds of America* (4 vols, London 1827–38). The 435 colour plates were engraved by Robert Havell.

27 Bonaparte's Gull from *The Birds of America,* 1827–38
hand coloured engraving
50.2 x 37.4
THE RUSKIN GALLERY, SHEFFIELD

Sir Charles Bell (1774–1842)

Physiologist, anatomist and surgeon. Discovered distinct functions of the nerves; illustrated his and his brother's anatomical works, and gave lessons in anatomy. Wrote *Anatomy of Expression* (1806) and a Bridgewater Treatise on the hand (1833); also illustrated Paley's *Natural Theology*. The drawings shown here are for his *Engravings of the Arteries.*

28 Drawings for Engravings of the Arteries
(i) **Pl. III showing arteries of the head.**
    22 x 14
(ii) **Pl. IV vertical section of head, showing arteries.**
    22.5 x 14
(iii) **Pl. VI showing the arteries of the arm.**
    15 x 23
watercolour
LIBRARY, ROYAL COLLEGE OF SURGEONS

Felix Bracquemond (1833–1914)

Painter and engraver; this is one of his most celebrated prints.

29 The Top half of a Door 1865
etching
27.8 x 38.3
THE HUNTERIAN ART GALLERY, UNIVERSITY OF GLASGOW

Arthur Burgess or Unknown photographer

Burgess was one of several artists whom Ruskin employed as copyists. These may be some of the photographs that Ruskin had Burgess take of the North West Porch of Rouen Cathedral. Gothic stone carving combined several themes in Ruskin's imagination: stone itself, fine craftsmanship and decoration based on living nature. (Compare Ruskin's own drawings shown here: the interrelationship of rock and vegetation, cat no 56,

30 Photographs of Rouen Cathedral: North West Porch
(i) **view of porch as a whole**
    40.5 x 30
(ii) **detail of left inner arch**
    39.1 x 29.9
(iii) **detail of left side**
    40.4 x 31.9
(iv) **detail of top left**
    39.6 x 29.2

the Gothic geometry of a peacock's feather, cat no 55.)

(v) **detail of the centre**
  38.2 x 29.5
silver prints

John Sell Cotman (1782–1842)

Chiefly a watercolourist and etcher, one of the Norwich school of landscape artists. Developed a Piranesi-like etching style which he used to particular advantage in interpreting the ruins and rock-masses of Normandy. *Castle of Falaise* was published as plate 90 in *Architectural Antiquities of Normandy*, 1822.

31 Castle of Falaise, North View 1821
etching
28.1 x 38.2
DR MICHAEL PIDGLEY

32 Grand Bonfire at the Yarmouth Festival
dated 19 April 1814
soft ground etching
17.8 x 26.3
NORFOLK MUSEUMS SERVICE (NORWICH CASTLE MUSEUM)

32

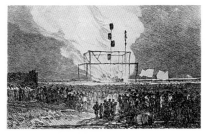

33 Brignall Banks on the Greta c1805
pencil and watercolour
18.7 x 28.9
LEEDS CITY ART GALLERIES

34 Brignall Banks on the Greta c1805
pencil
12.8 x 20.9
LEEDS CITY ART GALLERIES

Francis Danby (1792–1837)

A Dubliner who began his painting career in Bristol; the works shown here come from that early period. Like John Martin, he also painted visionary and fantastic landscapes.

35 St Vincent's Rocks from Nightingale Valley
1819
pencil and watercolour
21.3 x 32.1
CITY OF BRISTOL MUSEUM AND ART GALLERY

36 The Avon from Durdham Down 1821
watercolour and bodycolour
12.7 x 19.7
CITY OF BRISTOL MUSEUM AND ART GALLERY

37 The Avon at Clifton 1821
pencil, watercolour and bodycolour
12.9 x 21.7
CITY OF BRISTOL MUSEUM AND ART GALLERY

35

William Daniell (1769–1837)

Trained in watercolour and aquatint by his uncle, Thomas, with whom he produced *Oriental Scenery* (1795–1808). The works shown here come from his own series *A Voyage around Great Britain*, published in eight volumes, 1814–25, containing 308 aquatints.

38 The Cormorant's Cave, Staffa 1818
hand coloured aquatint
22.4 x 30.3
THE HUNTERIAN ART GALLERY, UNIVERSITY OF GLASGOW

39 View from the Island of Staffa 1818
hand coloured aquatint
22.6 x 30.3
THE HUNTERIAN ART GALLERY, UNIVERSITY OF GLASGOW

Maxime du Camp (1822–94)

Early photographer of Middle Eastern monuments. The photographs shown here come from *Egypte, Nubie, Palestine et Syrie…*, Paris 1852.

40
(i) **Colosse occidental du Speos de Phré**
22.8 x 16.2
(ii) **Grand Temple de Denderah**
Sculpture de la façade postérieure
15.7 x 21.9
(iii) **Grand Temple de Denderah**
Hypètre construit sur la Terrasse
16.1 x 21.9
salt prints
THE ROYAL PHOTOGRAPHIC SOCIETY

Francis Frith (1822–98)

Early topographical photographer, who published views taken on travels in the Middle East, 1856–1859.

41 Interior of the Hall of Columns, Karnak
from Album 'Lower Egypt, Thebes and the Pyramids' 1859
albumen print from wet collodion negative
22.6 x 15.6
THE ROYAL PHOTOGRAPHIC SOCIETY

42 Crocodile on a sand-bank
From Album 'Egypt, Sinai and Palestine' 1859
albumen print from wet collodion negative
15 x 21.8
THE ROYAL PHOTOGRAPHIC SOCIETY

William Henry Hunt (1790–1864)

Watercolourist admired by Ruskin and by his father, both of whom owned work by him.

43 Bank of Primroses and Blackthorn
watercolour and bodycolour on card
29.2 x 21.2
HARRIS MUSEUM AND ART GALLERY, PRESTON

William Holman Hunt (1827–1910)

A founder of the Pre-Raphaelite Brotherhood in 1848; travelled to Egypt and the Holy Land, partly in company with Thomas Seddon, in 1854–5. Hunt's landscape watercolours have a less elaborate narrative content than do his oil paintings, and yet they embody a search for meaning: the intense sunlight shows all that can merely be seen, and this is to prompt the viewer to extract unseen significance (see the entry for Seddon).

44 Distant View of Nazareth 1855
watercolour and bodycolour
35.3 x 49.8
WHITWORTH ART GALLERY, UNIVERSITY OF MANCHESTER

45 The Sphinx, Gizeh, Looking towards the Pyramids of Sakhara 1854
watercolour and bodycolour
25.4 x 35.5
HARRIS MUSEUM AND ART GALLERY, PRESTON

Charles Landseer (1795–1879)

Brother of Thomas and Edwin, and like them a painter. These drawings reflect the style and principles of Charles Bell, and were done when Landseer studied anatomy with him, as a young artist. Landseer became an RA in 1845 and was later Keeper in the RA Schools. He inherited Stubbs' drawings for the *Anatomy of the Horse* from Edwin, and bequeathed them in turn to the RA.

46 Muscles of neck and shoulder, and trachea
black, red and white chalk
35 x 29.3
WELLCOME INSTITUTE LIBRARY, LONDON

47 Right lateral view of trunk and neck of écorché corpse supine
black, red and white chalk
49.4 x 72.3
WELLCOME INSTITUTE LIBRARY, LONDON

Loewy and Puiseaux

The photographs were photoengraved and printed by L. Schutzenberger, Paris. Overlay sheets (not shown here) were added naming the features shown.

48 Plate XLVI of Photographie Lunaire 1903
photogravure
57 x 46.5
PRIVATE COLLECTION

Alexander Macdonald (c. 1839–1921)

Painter of still life and landscape, brought by Ruskin to the Oxford Drawing School in 1871.

49 A Study of Opal in Ferrugineous Jasper from New Guinea, 1884
watercolour and bodycolour
15 x 15.6
THE RUSKIN GALLERY, SHEFFIELD

John Martin (1789–1854)

Best known for his visionary paintings of earth-moving cataclysms.

50 The Wye Valley, view from Wyndcliffe looking towards Chepstow 1844
watercolour, surface scratching and pencil
30.3 x 72.1
WHITWORTH ART GALLERY, UNIVERSITY OF MANCHESTER

John Middleton (1828–56)

Landscape painter and engraver; also a photographer.

51 Dock Leaves c1847
watercolour
22.2 x 34.5
NORFOLK MUSEUMS SERVICE (NORWICH CASTLE MUSEUM)

John Everett Millais (1829–96)

Pre-Raphaelite; painted Ruskin amongst rocks and stream at Glenfinlas.

52 Study for 'Isabella' c1849
pencil
25.7 x 20
BIRMINGHAM CITY MUSEUMS AND ART GALLERY

Frank Randal (c1858–1901)

Employed by Ruskin as a copyist from 1881 to 1886.

53 Study of a spray of whortleberry 1882
watercolour and body colour on grey-blue ground
12.4 x 10.2
THE RUSKIN GALLERY, SHEFFIELD

John Ruskin (1819–1900)

Ruskin is central to the exhibition; in addition to his own watercolours there are pictures from the collection of the Guild of St George, including the Audubon and work that Ruskin commissioned or purchased from Burgess, Randal and Macdonald. Ruskin insisted on detailed accuracy partly for pedagogic reasons, and partly because his imagination pared everything down to structure, inner life: interstices, faults, lines of growth and force.

54 Coast Scene near Dunbar 1857
pen and ink and watercolour, touched with bodycolour
32.5 x 47.5
BIRMINGHAM CITY MUSEUMS AND ART GALLERY

55 Study of a Peacock's Feather – Dorsal Feather with its Analysis 1877
watercolour, bodycolour and pencil
14.3 x 9.5
THE RUSKIN GALLERY, SHEFFIELD

56 Study of Moss, Fern and Wood Sorrel and a Rocky Bank 1875–9
pencil and watercolour
14 x 24.8
THE RUSKIN GALLERY, SHEFFIELD

Thomas Matthew Rooke (1842–1942)

Rooke was one of the artists employed by Ruskin to make visual records of mediaeval buildings, whose destruction or damaging restoration Ruskin feared. After 1893, others paid for Rooke to continue his work against time.

57 West Front of the Church of Le Monastier, Haute Loire 1908
pencil and watercolour
83.5 x 66.8
BIRMINGHAM CITY MUSEUMS AND ART GALLERY

W Say (1768–1834)

A painter and a distinguished engraver; pupil of James Ward. He engraved these plates for Richard Bright's pioneering work in the science of pathology.

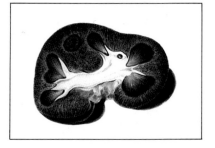

58(i)

58 Reports of Clinical Cases, drawn and engraved
1827
  (i) **plate 5, 1 figure of the kidney**
      after F R Say
      33.7 x 24.5
  (ii) **plate 1, 6 figures of the brain**
      after C J Canton 1830
      32.7 x 25
  (iii) **plate 10, 1 figure of a lung**
      after F R Say
      21 x 26.2
stipple engraving with watercolour
WELLCOME INSTITUTE LIBRARY, LONDON

Thomas Seddon (1821–1856)

Religious conversion inspired Seddon to visit the Holy Land in 1853, where Holman Hunt joined him. He died during a second visit to Egypt in 1856. *The Well of En-Rogel* refers to a Biblical episode in which two youths hide for safety in a well. The subject is characteristic of Seddon's and Hunt's attempt to discern the Biblical past under the surface they so searchingly rendered.

59 The Well of En-Rogel 1854–5
watercolour and bodycolour
25 x 35
HARRIS MUSEUM AND ART GALLERY, PRESTON

James Ward (1769–1859)

Painter of animal subjects; a man of deeply religious outlook, who admired Blake's work. Both exhibits relate to the painting of Gordale Scar commissioned by Lord Ribblesdale in 1811, and completed in 1814 (now in the Tate Gallery).

60 Study for Gordale Scar 1811–13
oil on canvas
38.1 x 55.9
LEEDS CITY ART GALLERIES

61 A Young Bull 1811
oil over pencil on paper, laid on canvas
30.5 x 43.2
WOLVERHAMPTON ART GALLERY AND MUSEUMS

William Ward (1766–1826) after Thomas Weaver (1774–1843)

William Ward, an engraver, reproduced paintings by his brother James Ward and other artists, including Weaver, a noted painter of animals.

62 A Short-horned heifer, 7 years old 1811
mezzotint
66 x 94
AGRICULTURAL ECONOMICS UNIT, OXFORD

3

ARTISTS BORN AFTER 1870

Ansel Adams (b1902)

Landscape photographer, particularly of the western United States; associate of Edward Weston from the 1930s onwards.

63 Frozen Lake and Cliffs, Sierra Nevada California 1927
silver print
35.5 x 45.8
THE TRUSTEES OF THE VICTORIA AND ALBERT MUSEUM

64 Aspens, New Mexico 1944
gelatin silver print
48.5 x 38.7
THE TRUSTEES OF THE VICTORIA AND ALBERT MUSEUM

Michael Andrews (b1928)

British figurative painter, whose images often tend to convey a paradoxical sense of unreality. This watercolour is part of a body of work made in response to Ayers Rock and the Olgas in Central Australia

65 Katatjuta (the Olgas; eastern domes) the apparent Colonnades 1984
watercolour
24.2 x 37.2
WHITWORTH ART GALLERY, UNIVERSITY OF MANCHESTER

Bernhard and Hilla Becher (b1931, 1934)

German photographers specialising in austere documentary views of industrial buildings. These are black and white photographs, of a regular format and generally exhibited in series according to building type.

66 I–IV Engine Houses, 1989
silver prints
40.5 x 48
VICTORIA MIRO GALLERY

Chuck Close (b1940)

One of the originators of the style most generally known as Photo-Realism, and included in group exhibitions with Richard Estes and others working in a similar vein, from 1964 onwards. As a movement, Photo-Realism did not outlast the 1970s, but Close's work – consistently based on passport-type photographs – continues to attract attention. Photo-Realism is a style that emerged from post-war American modernism; it refers only indirectly to the realism of earlier traditions.

67 Self-Portrait 1977
etching
113 x 90.2
THE TRUSTEES OF THE TATE GALLERY

Robert Cottingham (b1935)

One of the West Coast Photo-Realists, who tend to specialise in segments of commercial culture – the neon sign, in his case. By formally isolating these signs, and by emphasising facts of pure visibility, he suppresses meaning and reference.

68 Carl's 1977
etching
25.7 x 26.1

Richard Estes (b1936)

Like other Photo-Realists, Estes specialises in a particular subject-matter; in his case, debased urban scenes, chosen as foils to art itself, rather than for any social motive. The challenge for the artist is to make the over-familiar and banal become strange. The painting or – as in this case – screenprint differs from the photograph not only in scale and medium, but also by showing a consistent sharpness of focus.

69 Holland Hotel 1984
screenprint
115 x 183.2

Richard Eurich (b1903)

A British painter who, like Algernon Newton and McIntosh Patrick, developed a highly individual, non-modernist landscape style.

70 The Watercourse, Gordale 1949
oil on canvas
102.6 x 102.3

Lucian Freud (b1922)

Grandson of Sigmund Freud; came to England with his family as a refugee in 1933. He already drew prolifically, in a style informed by German traditions; this, as Lawrence Gowing's account suggests (*Lucian Freud,* London 1982), put him at a double distance from his adoptive culture. His recent work, while being formidably concerned with realities of physical presence, conveys an equally strong sense of unreality: of not being at home.

71 Still Life with Sea Urchin 1949
tempera on panel
30.8 x 24.7

72 Bananas 1963
oil on canvas
23 x 15

73 The Painter's Mother 1982
etching
17.8 x 15.2

74 Man Posing 1985
etching
70 x 55

Charles Ginner (1878–1952)

75 **Rame Head, Cornwall** 1924
pen, ink and watercolour
23.8 x 30.5
BRADFORD ART GALLERIES AND MUSEUMS

David Hepher (b1935)

Like some Photo-Realists, he finds a strange beauty in unloved architecture; though in his case through discernment, and by way of allusion to earlier art – latterly, to Piranesi's visionary etchings of prisons.

76 **Camberwell Nocturne** 1984
oil on canvas
210 x 240
ANGELA FLOWERS GALLERY

Frank Hurley (1885–1962)

An Australian who took photographs on five Antarctic expeditions, including Shackleton's expedition of 1914–17, when the *Endurance* was crushed by ice.

77(v)

78(ii)

77 **From the Imperial Trans-Antarctic Expedition 1914–17 on the** *Endurance* **led by Ernest Shackleton**
(i) **The pack illumined by the Low Winter Sun (The Departing Seas)** 1913
29 x 36
(ii) **The Launching of the** *James Caird*
38 x 51
(iii) **Exercising the dogs –** *Endurance* **frozen in the Weddell Sea**
18 x 23.5
(iv) **Within a few seconds she heeled over, she had a list of 30° to Port**
23.5 x 18
(v) **Ice pressure approaching the ship: the** *Endurance* **at mid Winter. Photographed by the light of a burning oil drum in the bows and magnesium flash (***Endurance* **trapped in the Ice)**
18 x 23.5
gelatine prints
THICKETS COLLECTION

78 **From the Imperial Trans-Antarctic Expedition 1914–1917 on the** *Endurance* **led by Ernest Shackleton**
(i) **The night watchman returns** 1915
(ii) **The cliffs of the Hamburg Glacier, Moraine Fjord, South Georgia** 1914
(iii) **Members of the expedition on the frozen Weddell Sea** 1915

(iv) **Ship's Cabin** 1915
silver prints
16.5 x 20.5
ROYAL GEOGRAPHICAL SOCIETY

79 From the British and New Zealand Antarctic Expedition 1929/31: Sphinx Rock near Rogers Head, Heard Island
silver print
20.5 x 16.5
ROYAL GEOGRAPHICAL SOCIETY
78(iv)

Thomas Lowinsky (1892–1947)

Painted surrealist-inspired fantasies as well as hyper-real portraits, in both cases using tempera to precise effect.

80 Portrait of Miss Cecily Hamilton 1926
tempera on board
22.9 x 25.4
SHEFFIELD CITY ART GALLERIES

Rory McEwen (1932–1982)

A botanical artist with a parallel commitment to modern art; McEwen worked on vellum, in the tradition of artists like Ehret, to whose paintings he was introduced by his teacher at Eton, Wilfrid Blunt (then writing *The Art of Botanical Illustration*).

81 Limerston Street 1979
watercolour on vellum
46 x 56.5
PRIVATE COLLECTION

82 Dutchman's Farm, Eton 1979
watercolour on vellum
39.5 x 34.2
PRIVATE COLLECTION

Henry Moore OM (1898–1986)

Shown here are five of the 28 numbered etchings that Moore published in his Elephant Skull album, 1969-70

83 Elephant Skull
(i) **Plate X** 1970
     29.8 x 20
(ii) **Plate XIX** 1969
     23.5 x 30.8
(iii) **Plate XX** 1969
     23.5 x 21.6
(iv) **Plate XXIV** 1970
     20 x 29.8
(v) **Plate XXV** 1970
     23.5 x 27.9
etching
THE HENRY MOORE FOUNDATION

National Aeronautical and Space Agency, USA

84

(i) **Challenger VI 1984: the Grand Canyon of Colorado**

(ii) **Apollo Saturn II 1969: Earth above the surface of the Moon**

(iii) **Apollo 19 1972: Earth from the Landing Site, Moon rock in Foreground**

prints from transparencies

TRANSPARENCIES LENT BY NASA

Algernon Newton (1880–1968)

Produced notably haunting urban landscapes that, while modern in sensibility, owe nothing to modernism.

85 **The Backs of Houses, Harley Street** 1925

oil on canvas

27 x 49.5

THE MUSEUM OF LONDON

86 **Vicarage Gate, Kensington (From my Studio Window)** 1948–49

oil on canvas

90 x 120

PRIVATE COLLECTION

James McIntosh Patrick (b. 1907)

In the context of this exhibition, Patrick's is a notably benign vision of the human and natural world, Brueghel-like in its high viewpoint and inclusiveness.

87 **A City Garden** 1940

oil on canvas

71.1 x 91.4

DUNDEE ART GALLERIES AND MUSEUMS

Herbert Ponting (1871–1935)

Took photographs in Japan, which he published in two books, before going as official photographer with Scott's second Antarctic expedition, 1910–12. Produced a film as well as many photographs, some of which he reproduced in his book *The Great White South* 1921.

88 **Ice Grotto and the *Terra Nova*** 1910–12

gelatin silver print

35.4 x 22.8

THE TRUSTEES OF THE VICTORIA & ALBERT MUSEUM

Albert Renger-Patzsch (1897–1966)

Participant in German *Neue Sachlichkeit* (New Objectivity) movement of the 1920's; this remained evident in a vision that assimilated creations of nature to artefacts, or endowed objects with enhanced presence.

90

89 Heterotrichum macrodum c 1924
gelatin silver print
28.2 x 38.1

90 Crab-fisherwoman (from the book *Halligen* 1924)
gelatin silver print
38.1 x 28.3

91 Measuring and Mixing Cylinders 1932 (printed 1938)
gelatin silver print
25 x 18.6

92 Stirrer 1934 (printed 1978)
gelatin silver print
24.8 x 18.6

Edwin Smith (1912–1971)

In early life a builder, then an apprentice architect, he began to take photographs during the 1930s, first concentrating on circus and fairground subjects. Later, he produced remarkably sympathetic photographs of architecture, published in books during the 1950s and 60s.

93 Buckinghamshire, Quainton, Winwood Monument 1689 by Thomas Stainer
gelatin silver print
25.3 x 20.3

94 Ambulatory of the Crypt, Canterbury 1968
gelatin silver print
25.3 x 20.3

95 Didmarton Church, Gloucester 1961
gelatin silver print
20 x 25

96 Bantry House, Co Cork, Ireland 1965
25.3 x 20.3 gelatin silver print

Sir Stanley Spencer (1891–1959)

In their sobriety of style, the works shown here contrast with Spencer's visionary images. While there was certainly a financial motive for painting 'realistically' he did paint in this manner some pictures that clearly had personal significance. It is as if he were putting to trial his own religious faith – by taking the measure of things as they are.

97

97 The Boatbuilder's Yard 1936
oil on canvas
86.8 x 71.4
MANCHESTER CITY ART GALLERIES

98 Helter Skelter 1937
oil on canvas
91.5 x 58.5
SHEFFIELD CITY ART GALLERIES

99 Landscape in North Wales 1938
oil on canvas
55.9 x 70.8
THE SYNDICS OF THE FITZWILLIAM MUSEUM, CAMBRIDGE

100 Portrait of Margaret Pilkington 1953
pencil and pen and ink
35.7 x 25.4
WHITWORTH ART GALLERY, UNIVERSITY OF MANCHESTER

Edward Weston (1886–1958)

American photographer, associated with Alfred Stieglitz, Tina Modotti, Ansel Adams (see above). Worked in California and in Mexico; as a photographer of landscape he was a notable interpreter of desert and waste.

101
(i) **Point Lobos** 1930
  printed by Cole Weston
  24 x 19.1
(ii) **Point Lobos** 1946
  printed by Cole Weston
  24.2 x 19
(iii) **Excusado, Mexico** 1926
  printed by Cole Weston
  24.1 x 18.7
gelatin silver prints
THE TRUSTEES OF THE VICTORIA AND ALBERT MUSEUM

LIST OF LENDERS

James Kirkman Ltd **73, 74**
Dr Michael Pidgley **31**
The Thickets Collection **77**
Private collections **81, 82, 86**
The Royal Photographic Society, Bath **40–42, 89, 90**
Birmingham City Museums and Art Gallery **16, 52, 54, 57**
Bradford Art Galleries and Museums **75**
Royal Pavilion, Art Gallery and Museum, Brighton **25**
City of Bristol Museum and Art Gallery **35–37**
The Syndics of the Fitzwilliam Museum, Cambridge **17, 99**
Dundee Art Galleries and Museums **87**
The Hunterian Art Gallery, University of Glasgow **21, 23, 24, 29, 38, 39**
The Librarian, Glasgow University **19**
Leeds City Art Galleries **10, 33, 34, 60**
Ken and Jenny Jacobson **48**

London:
Angela Flowers Gallery **76**
Hazlitt, Gooden & Fox Ltd. **9, 12, 26**
The Museum of London **85**
Royal Academy of Arts **20**
Royal College of Surgeons, Hunterian Collection **28**
The Royal Geographical Society **78, 79**
The Trustees of the British Museum (Natural History) Botany Library **1 to 7**
The Trustees of the Tate Gallery **67–69**
The Trustees of the Victoria and Albert Museum **63, 64, 88, 91–96, 101**
Victoria Miro Gallery **66**
Wellcome Institute Library, London **11, 13 to 15, 18, 46, 47, 58**

Manchester City Art Galleries **97**
Whitworth Art Gallery, University of Manchester **44, 50, 65, 100**
The Henry Moore Foundation, Much Hadham **83**
NASA, Houston, Texas, USA **84**
Norfolk Museums Service (Norwich Castle Museum) **32, 51**
Agricultural Economics Unit, Oxford **8, 22, 62**
Harris Museum and Art Gallery, Preston **43, 45, 59, 70, 71**
Sheffield City Art Galleries **80, 98**
Sheffield, The Ruskin Gallery **27, 30, 49, 53, 55, 56**
Southampton City Art Gallery **72**
Wolverhampton Art Gallery and Museums **61**

Photographs are all courtesy the lenders.
(Cat. no. 77(v), John Webb; Cat. Nos. 8, 22 and 62, Jim Chambers)

Exhibition organised by
Caroline Collier and Elizabeth Knowles
assisted by
Wendy Hepper and Jill Porter

Catalogue designed by
Grundy & Northedge Designers

Printed by
Dot for Dot Printers Ltd

Cover illustration:
John Russell
Plate from Lunar Planispheres 1805–6
Cat no. 18

Catalogue title illustration: Impey Collection
brown and pale yellow snake 1782
Cat no. 13 (ii)

ISBN 1 85332 0641

A full list of Arts Council
and South Bank Centre publications
may be obtained from:
The Publications Office,
South Bank Centre,
Royal Festival Hall,
Belvedere Road,
London SE1 8XX